JULIUS CAESAR

First published in North America in 2007 by the
National Geographic Society
1145 17th Street N.W.
Washington, D.C. 20036-4688

Copyright © 2007 Marshall Editions
A Marshall Edition
Conceived, edited, and designed by Marshall Editions
The Old Brewery, 6 Blundell Street, London N7 9BH, U.K.
www.quarto.com

Trade ISBN: 978-1-4263-0064-6   *3658   7627   12/07*
Library ISBN: 978-1-4263-0065-3
Library of Congress Cataloging-in-Publication Data available on request.

Originated in Hong Kong by Modern Age
Printed and bound in China by Midas Printing Limited

Publisher: Richard Green
Commissioning editor: Claudia Martin
Art direction: Ivo Marloh
Picture manager: Veneta Bullen
Production: Anna Pauletti

Consultant: Professor Mary Beard
Design and editorial: Tall Tree Ltd.
Picture research: Caroline Wood

For the National Geographic Society:
Design director: Bea Jackson
Project editor: Priyanka Lamichhane

One of the world's largest nonprofit scientific and educational organizations, the National Geographic Society was founded in 1888 "for the increase and diffusion of geographic knowledge." Fulfilling this mission, the Society educates and inspires millions every day through its magazines, books, television programs, videos, maps and atlases, research grants, the National Geographic Bee, teacher workshops, and innovative classroom materials. The Society is supported through membership dues, charitable gifts, and income from the sale of its educational products. This support is vital to National Geographic's mission to increase global understanding and promote conservation of our planet through exploration, research, and education.

For more information, please call 1-800-NGS LINE (647-5463) or write to the following address:

NATIONAL GEOGRAPHIC SOCIETY
1145 17th Street N.W.
Washington, D.C. 20036-4688 U.S.A.

Visit the Society's Web site at www.nationalgeographic.com.

Previous page: Julius Caesar shown on a silver coin. He was the first living person to appear on a Roman coin.

Opposite: A bronze figurine from the 1st century A.D. shows an army standard-bearer proudly holding up a pole topped with an eagle, the symbol of Roman power.

JULIUS CAESAR

THE BOY WHO CONQUERED AN EMPIRE

ELLEN GALFORD

NATIONAL GEOGRAPHIC

WASHINGTON, D.C.

CONTENTS

A ROMAN HERO'S EARLY DAYS

1

COMING OF AGE

2

THE WARRIOR

3

HAIL, CAESAR!

4

A ROMAN HERO'S EARLY DAYS

Birth of a Conqueror

At the dawn of the first century B.C., Rome was the biggest city in the world and controlled a vast empire that stretched from modern-day France to North Africa. The city was home to hundreds of thousands of people, rich and poor, slaves and aristocrats. One day in around the year 100 B.C., a baby was born in the city who would become famous the world over. He was named Gaius Julius Caesar.

Gaius Julius Caesar was born into an aristocratic family. They were one of a small group of families who had owned the land that became Rome and had lived in the city since it was founded. For centuries, these families had made almost all the decisions about how Rome should be run. Caesar's parents were not very wealthy, but they had enough money to live comfortably. They lived in quite a large house in a crowded neighborhood called the Subura.

The day of the baby's arrival would have been a frightening time for his parents. Childbirth was always dangerous, with little that a midwife or a doctor could do if things went wrong. Many new mothers—and their babies—died. According to legend, Caesar's birth was difficult, but both he and his mother survived.

Previous page: This bronze sculpture of a young Roman boy dates from a few years before Gaius Julius Caesar's birth.

Lighting the way
Romans often placed lighted candles around the bed of a woman in childbirth, to chase away evil spirits. They hoped that this would keep both mother and baby safe.

Due to the problem of dating events in ancient Rome, some dates are approximate. "c." is an abbreviation of "circa," meaning "about."

753 B.C.
According to ancient tradition, Rome is founded.

According to custom, when the baby was a few minutes old, the midwife who had helped at the birth would have lifted him from his mother's arms and placed him on the floor at his father's feet. The father would have held up the baby, to show that he had accepted the child into the family.

Caesar, like all Romans of his class, received three names at birth. His first name was Gaius, after his father. This was the name that his family would have used. Julius referred to the clan—the Julii—to which his ancestors belonged. Caesar was rather like our surname.

Below: Carved figures on a Roman tomb show moments of happy family life. A father watches his wife nurse their newborn child, and then he holds the baby in his arms.

I07 B.C.

Gaius Julius Caesar's uncle Marius—political leader and war hero—reorganizes the Roman army.

c. I02–I00 B.C.

Gaius Julius Caesar, son of Gaius Julius Caesar and Aurelia, is born in Rome.

Caesar's Childhood

While Gaius's father served the Roman Republic as a magistrate, his mother, Aurelia, took charge of her baby's upbringing. Like other Roman mothers of her class, she had slaves to do the hard work in the house and to help with day-to-day childcare.

As Gaius moved from babyhood to childhood, he would have spent his days in the same way as any other Roman boy growing up in a comfortable home. He wore a loose, knee-length tunic made of white wool or linen, trimmed with a band of red. Girls wore tunics too, but fastened with a belt around the waist. When they left the house, children covered themselves with a second, longer

tunic that reached down to their ankles.

Up until the age of six or seven, Gaius probably had plenty of free time to play. Roman toys included carved animals, rocking horses, balls, marbles made of pottery or brightly colored glass, and many different kinds of board games, including early versions of chess and checkers.

Left: In a relief carved by a 1st-century A.D. sculptor, Roman boys wearing short, loose tunics test their strength in a wrestling match that may have started out as fun but looks as if it might get serious.

100 B.C.
Caesar's uncle Marius is elected consul of Rome for the sixth time.

98 B.C.
The Roman philosopher Lucretius is born. His book *On the Nature of Things* will describe particles called atoms.

Right: This carving on the tomb of a little boy shows him steering a tiny chariot pulled by a donkey, pretending to be one of the charioteers whose races thrilled all of Rome.

There were also dolls made of cloth, wood, wax, or clay.

Battle games were always popular. Outdoors, groups of playmates split up into teams for a round of "the Troy game" (named after the famous ancient battle of Troy), in which players tried to drag their opponents across a line drawn on the ground. Gaius might also have amused himself for hours, alone or with a companion, using wooden swords and child-size helmets for waging make-believe warfare.

Gaius might have received some of these toys as birthday presents. The Romans took these occasions seriously and loved to celebrate with special gifts, as well as parties for family and friends. And in an age when medicine was limited and it was all too common for children to die young, the fact that a son or daughter had survived for another year was a good reason for celebration. Gaius's own family had suffered the loss of a child. He had two older sisters, one of whom died while he was just a baby. We do not know the girls' first names, but the one who grew up alongside him had a second name—Julia—that was the female version of her brother's.

c. 97 B.C.
One of Caesar's two older sisters dies.

96 B.C.
The last king of Cyrenacia—now Libya—in North Africa dies. In his will, he leaves his kingdom to Rome.

Left: This metal tag hung around the neck of a slave, identifying its wearer as a piece of property. Children of slave parents were slaves from birth. Some became playmates for their owner's children. Others had to work in the household as soon as they were big enough to fetch and carry, or they were sold to another master.

Aurelia was a loving parent, but a strict one. According to tradition, many of Rome's greatest citizens owed their achievements to the mothers who had molded them into heroes. Officially all the power in a household might have rested with the father, but mothers like Aurelia could be strong characters in their own right. Such women prided themselves on their modesty and piety, but they took no nonsense from anyone.

Every Roman family who could afford to own slaves used them to do all the heavy labor in the home. Slaves also toiled without pay in the fields, workshops, and warehouses. They were seen as property rather than as people, with no rights of any kind. Men, women, and children became slaves when their tribes or their homelands were defeated in war. Others were kidnapped by pirates and auctioned off to slave traders or—in some places— were enslaved as punishment for crimes. It was possible for slaves to gain their liberty if they could find a way to buy themselves out of slavery.

95 B.C.
Cato the Younger, who will grow up to become one of Caesar's fiercest critics, is born.

c. 94 B.C.
Caesar begins his schooling.

Among wealthy people like the Julii who owned land in the countryside, much of the food and wine they served at their tables would have been harvested on their own farms. Poorer city-dwellers, living in cramped apartments without kitchens of their own, could buy ready-made dishes from a store. Rome's markets were well stocked with many varieties of fish, fresh meat, and vegetables and fruits grown near the city. The Romans liked strong flavors. They used dozens of different herbs, olives, pungent cheeses, and a salty sauce made of carefully aged fish, which may have helped disguise the smell of foods that spoiled quickly in warm weather. Sugar was unknown, but sweet-toothed Romans satisfied their cravings by using lots of honey. Bakers in every neighborhood supplied fresh bread made from wheat, which, for Romans, was the most important basic food.

Above: A wall painting from a house in Pompeii, a town south of Rome that was buried by an erupting volcano in the first century A.D., shows an array of the fish and game birds that wealthy Romans loved to feast on.

Keeping a pet

Roman children often kept tame mice as pets. They hitched them up to tiny wooden carts light enough for the mice to pull around a room.

92 B.C.

The Romans invade Armenia, beginning a century of war between Rome and the Persian kings.

91 B.C.

Italian cities rebel against Rome, demanding citizenship rights. Rome refuses, starting the Social War.

A Roman House

Wealthy Romans lived in comfortable and often beautifully decorated homes. Houses were built from stone or brick and roofed with clay tiles. In crowded towns and cities, such as Rome itself, the houses of the rich generally turned their backs on the street, revealing mostly blank walls pierced with a few tiny windows. Inside, rooms opened onto a central courtyard—the atrium—and, at the rear, to a walled garden. People of more modest means often lived in apartment buildings, similar to those in modern cities. These structures had shops on the first floor and could rise as high as seven stories, with one or more families housed on every floor. Some of these blocks were solidly built, while others—especially in slum districts—were shaky firetraps that often tumbled down.

Above: In country towns, such as Pompeii, the homes of the wealthiest citizens, like the rich villa pictured here in a painting, sprawled over large tracts of land, with walled gardens and columned porches positioned to get the best breezes and the finest views.

LATRINES

Rome's plumbing system was more advanced than that of any city until modern times. Pipes made of lead or pottery carried a constant flow of fresh water to public wells and drinking fountains, and to the bathhouses where Romans went to wash. These pipes also fed into rich people's houses, allowing the use of a simple form of flushing toilet. Sewage pipes drained dirty water away. In apartment buildings, where less wealthy people lived, the water supply was only at street level. Anyone living on the upper floors either visited public lavatories like the one pictured here, or relied on chamber pots at home. When full, these had to be carried downstairs and emptied into the public sewer.

Below: Roman houses were dark at night, lit only by the flickering flames from small ceramic or metal lamps filled with burning olive oil.

Above: Rich Romans slept, and often dined, on luxurious beds and couches encrusted with gems and ivory. The bed shown here stands in a chamber decorated with colorful frescoes, dating from around the time of Caesar.

Schooldays

Wealthy Romans valued knowledge and education. They would have sent their sons, and sometimes their daughters, to school. Poorer children would have helped their parents around the house or in their trades.

Wealthy young boys attended small elementary schools that were usually run by a single teacher. Here they were taught simple arithmetic and how to read and write in their own language—Latin. Girls, destined for lives as wives and mothers, left school at age 11, if they were allowed to go at all. Boys spent

another few years at secondary school, studying history, geography, astronomy, music, mathematics, grammar, Greek and Roman literature, and athletics. In very wealthy households, educated slaves served as private tutors.

At the age of six or seven, young Gaius began his education.

Left: A boy, sculpted in marble on a Roman tomb, recites his lessons to a man who is either his father or his tutor. Both hold written scrolls of rolled-up sheets of papyrus, made from a reed-like plant.

90 B.C.
The Roman consul L. Julius Caesar passes a law giving citizenship to residents of cities not fighting Rome.

c. 89 B.C.
Caesar's father arranges for Gaius to become engaged to Cossutia, daughter of a rich, but not aristocratic, family.

Like many aristocratic Romans, his family turned to a foreigner to supervise Gaius's schooling. Many tutors were Greeks, admired by the Romans for their knowledge of the arts and sciences. Caesar's teacher, Marcus Antonius Gnipho, had been born in Gaul, the vast tribal lands to the north of Roman territory, but brought up in Greece. Gnipho was a gifted educator and respected scholar. He quickly realized that his pupil was highly intelligent, with a gift for language, a quick wit, a curiosity about the world, and a keen interest in observing people. With Gnipho's help, Caesar grew up to become an impressive public speaker and a successful author.

A talented writer

Gaius Julius Caesar showed his writing talents from an early age, composing poetry and plays. It was said that, while still a schoolboy, he wrote a long poem about the strongman Hercules, a superhero from ancient mythology.

Caesar probably continued his studies with Gnipho until he was about 16. Caesar was not Gnipho's only famous student. One of Caesar's contemporaries, Marcus Tullius Cicero, studied rhetoric with Gnipho when he was an adult and became one of the greatest orators in the history of Rome.

Right: Children learned to write on beeswax tablets, using a long, pointed pen called a stylus (pictured), made of ivory or metal. The pots were for ink, which was used for writing on papyrus.

88 B.C.
The Social War ends.

87 B.C.
Marius and Cinna become the two consuls governing Rome.

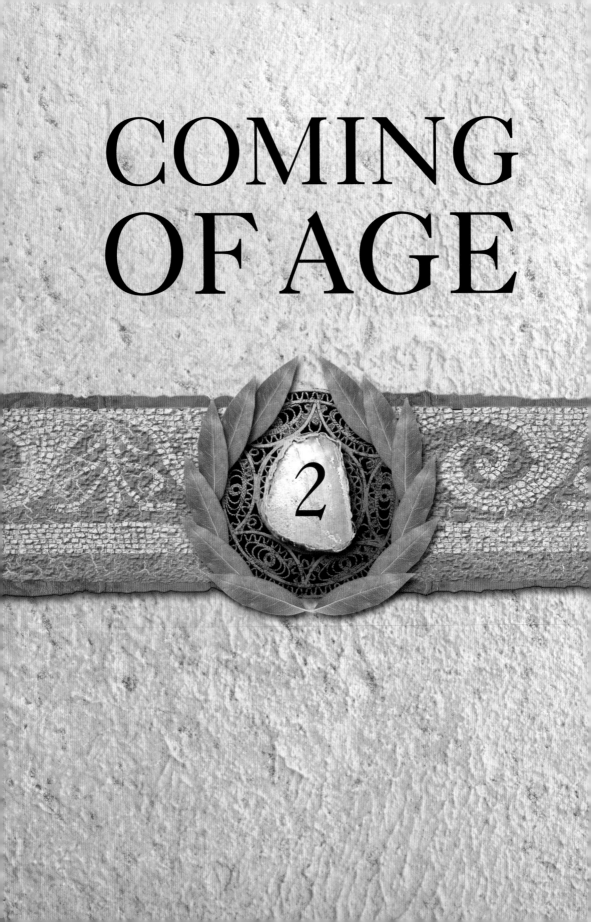

COMING OF AGE

2

A Roman Youth

When Gaius turned 16, according to Roman custom he officially became an adult. He was now entitled to wear a toga—the long, draped cloth that identified him as a Roman citizen. However, what should have been a year of celebration was also a sad time, with the sudden death of Gaius's father while he was away on business.

Gaius was now officially the head of the family, responsible for the welfare of his sister, Julia, and his widowed mother. He would remain close to his mother for the rest of her life, and she would share his home until she died.

Rome was an exciting place for a young man to enjoy his first taste of independence. The city was full of interesting things to do. The forum, the great public square at the heart of Rome, provided plenty of scope for people-watching. The city's streets were full of small shops. Caesar might have visited booksellers to browse among scrolls of poetry, history, or Greek philosophy.

Previous page: This bust of Julius Caesar as a young man was made during his lifetime or soon after he died.

Right: A mosaic from the 1st century A.D. shows the outcome of a violent duel between two gladiators. The winner kneels by the head of his fallen opponent, while the referee raises his right arm to declare the victory. Throughout their history, Romans loved these violent contests, along with chariot races, wild-animal acts, and other public spectacles, which took place in amphitheaters.

87 B.C.
King Mithridates of Pontus sweeps through Asia Minor attempting to drive all Romans out of the region.

c. 87 B.C.
Caesar is appointed a priest of Jupiter.

He might have attended public lectures by the great orators of the day, practiced his swordsmanship, and attended the theater or public spectacles such as chariot races and gladiatorial games. Caesar was always interested in meeting people. He had a gift for making—and keeping—friends. Men and, in particular, women found him a charming and attractive companion.

He was a good-looking youth, with dark, intelligent eyes. Two Roman historians, writing long after Caesar's lifetime, disagree about his appearance. Suetonius (c. A.D. 69–130) says that he was "tall, fair, and well-built," while Plutarch (c. A.D. 46–127) insists that he was small and slender. It is also said that he became bald when still a very young man. We know that Caesar liked to add unusual touches to his clothing, such as a tunic fitted with long, fringed sleeves. The Romans often judged character by how someone dressed. Some Romans criticized Caesar for wearing his belt much too loosely around his waist. They said this showed he was a man who could not be trusted.

Right: Romans visited public bathhouses, such as this one, as part of their daily routine. Bathhouses offered hot and cold plunge pools, steam rooms for relaxation, and quiet corners where friends could meet.

87 B.C.

Caesar's uncle Marius and his rival Sulla struggle for power, leading to bloodshed on the streets of Rome.

86 B.C.

After being elected consul for the seventh time, Marius dies.

The Roman World

By the time of Julius Caesar's birth around 100 B.C., the Romans controlled most of the lands on the European shores of the Mediterranean Sea, with a large territory in North Africa as well. Where Roman armies had conquered, Roman governors and merchants followed. Many different kingdoms became Roman provinces, owing loyalty and paying taxes to their new Roman masters. Caesar's native city served as the hub of a vast network of trade routes, with products and information flowing in all directions. During Julius Caesar's lifetime, Roman power was destined to reach even farther in all directions. After his death, Rome was able to extend its borders farther still, stretching as far north as Hadrian's Wall in Britain and including large stretches of North Africa and the Middle East.

Below: As the republic of the city of Rome turned into a major international power, its citizens liked to tell stories of their community's ancient beginnings. They traced their origins to a tribe called the Latins, who emerged from the mists of time in around 1000 B.C. to settle on the banks of the Tiber River, the future site of Rome. According to legend, Roman history began with a pair of twins named Romulus and Remus. Their mother was the daughter of a tribal ruler, while their father was said to be the god Mars. As infants, they were lost in the wilderness. However, as shown by the sculpture on top of this Roman column, a she-wolf rescued them. She fed and cared for them as if they were her own cubs. They grew up into brave heroes and built the city of Rome.

HADRIAN'S WALL

BRITAIN

ENGLISH CHANNEL

GAUL

Orange
Nimes
PONT DU GARD

SPAIN

Straits of Gibraltar

NORTH

KEY

The Roman Empire at Caesar's birth c. 100 B.C.

The Roman Empire at its farthest extent c. A.D. 117

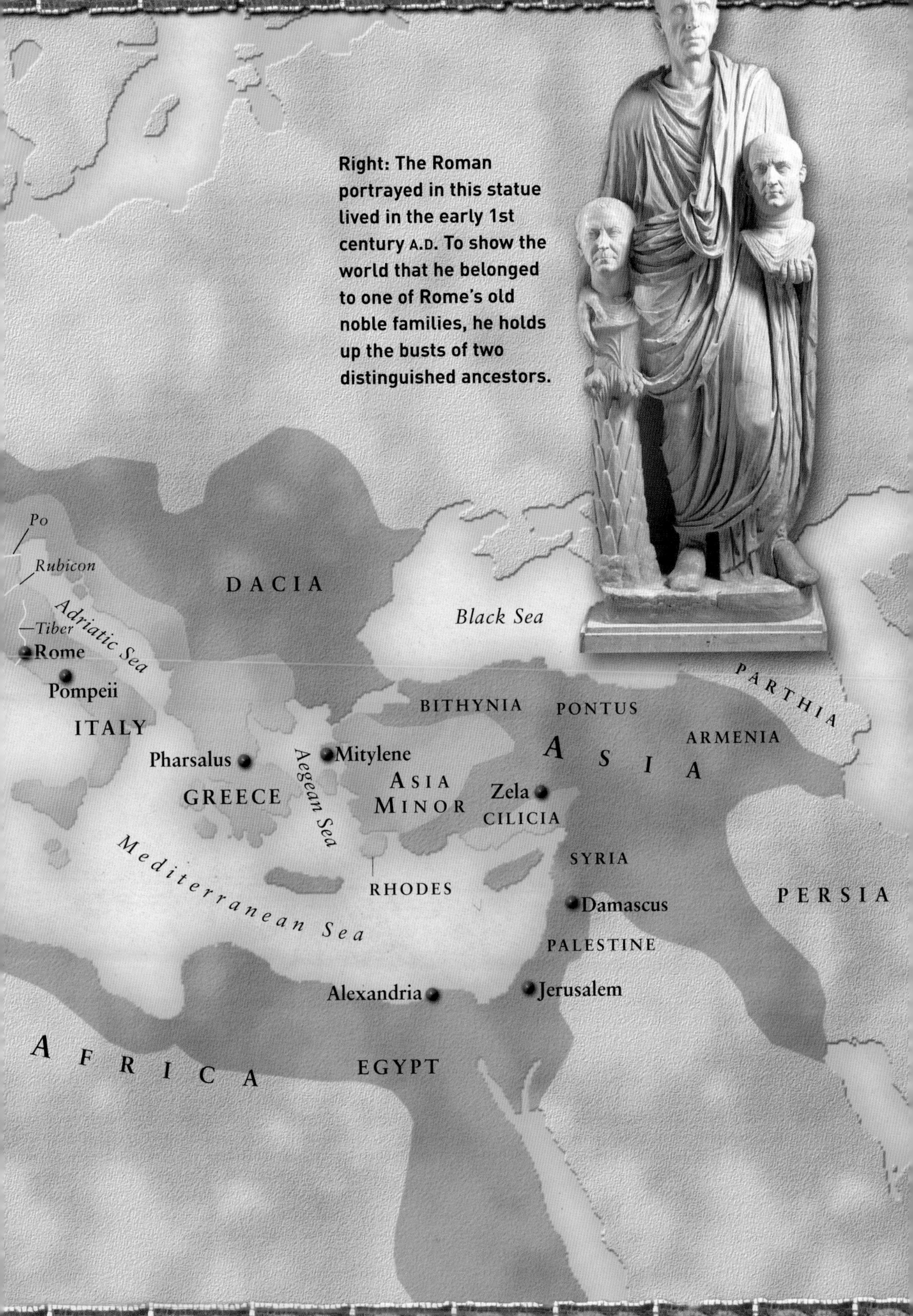

Right: The Roman portrayed in this statue lived in the early 1st century A.D. To show the world that he belonged to one of Rome's old noble families, he holds up the busts of two distinguished ancestors.

Po

Rubicon

DACIA

Black Sea

Adriatic Sea

Tiber

Rome

Pompeii

ITALY

PARTHIA

Pharsalus

GREECE

Aegean Sea

Mitylene

ASIA MINOR

BITHYNIA

PONTUS

A S I A

ARMENIA

Zela

CILICIA

RHODES

SYRIA

Damascus

PALESTINE

Jerusalem

PERSIA

Mediterranean Sea

Alexandria

AFRICA

EGYPT

Love and Marriage

Roman nobles did not see marriage as a match between a man and a woman in love but as a match between two families. If a Roman father wanted to strengthen his friendships with powerful men in the city, a good way to do it was to offer his daughter as a bride for one of their sons. Fathers sometimes forced children into marriages they did not want, but others tried to arrange matches that would make their children happy.

Long before his death, Caesar's father had chosen a bride for his son. Gaius, while he was still a boy, had been formally engaged to a young girl named Cossutia. However, once his father died, everything changed.

Gaius had an aunt on his father's side called Julia. She was the widow of Marius, the famous and successful army general. Marius had reformed the army, won an important war in North Africa, and beaten back an invasion by warlike tribes from Gaul, in present-day France. This last victory made him a national hero. People called him "the Third Founder of Rome."

Right: A Roman lady, carved in relief, takes a leisurely look at what is either a jewelry box or a case with a mirror in its lid, held up by a slave girl.

85 B.C.
Sulla persuades Rome's enemy, King Mithridates of Pontus, to sign a peace treaty in Asia Minor.

c. 84 B.C.
Caesar officially becomes an adult on his 16th birthday. His father dies.

Even after Marius's death, Aunt Julia still had a lot of friends in high places. She decided to use her influence to help her nephew succeed in life. She persuaded young Gaius to break off his engagement with Cossutia. She offered him another bride, with much better family connections.

Gaius, though barely 17, was already ambitious. He knew a good opportunity when he saw one, so shortly after breaking off with Cossutia he married the 13-year-old Cornelia. She was the daughter of Cinna, an important politician and the most powerful man in Rome.

This marriage helped Gaius take his first steps toward a career in politics, but it was more than just a useful match. The young couple actually grew to care for each other, and before long they became the proud parents of a baby girl. They named her Julia.

Wedding customs

Many modern marriage customs are surprisingly similar to those of ancient Rome. Wedding processions with bridesmaids, and brides wearing veils were all part of Roman weddings. Roman grooms also carried the bride over the threshold of their home.

Right: This golden armband crafted in the shape of a snake was found in the ruined Roman city of Pompeii, buried by a volcanic eruption in A.D. 79. It may have belonged to a wealthy woman who died in the disaster.

c. 84 B.C.
Caesar marries Cornelia, daughter of the consul Cinna.

84 B.C.
Cinna is murdered.

Dangerous Times

Young nobles, such as Caesar, were expected to play their part in government. When Gaius took his first steps into politics, Rome was a city at war with itself. Groups of people with very different needs and interests struggled for power, while angry mobs rioted in the streets. Caesar would have to step carefully if he was going to succeed.

In Caesar's time, Rome was a republic. Its people had governed themselves for 500 years. The city was controlled by the senate—a body of 600 citizens belonging to the city's oldest and most important land-owning families. Two senior officials, known as consuls, were elected by the citizens every year. It was the consuls' job to oversee the work of the senate and the Roman army. They were the most important people in the republic until their terms were over, and they had many advantages.

Right: This bronze statue from the 1st century B.C. shows Aulus Metellus, a Roman official who lived at the same time as Julius Caesar, delivering a speech. He raises one arm high to make an important point.

83 B.C.
Sulla, a rival of Caesar's uncle Marius, returns as a hero after military and diplomatic success in Asia.

c. 83 B.C.
Cornelia gives birth to Caesar's daughter, Julia.

Right: A silver coin from the Roman Republic shows a citizen voting by placing a piece of wood, coated in wax, into a jar. If this were an election to choose an officeholder, he would have used a stylus to write the name of his chosen candidate on the wax. If it were a vote to decide on a particular question, he would have marked it simply "yes" or "no."

They could reward their friends and followers by appointing them to military commands, and make sure that things were run in ways that would make their supporters happy.

Sometimes the senators felt that Rome was in grave danger, either from foreign enemies or from rebels inside its own boundaries. To protect the republic during these crises, the consuls would appoint one very strong leader to rule alone. This ruler would be given the title of "dictator," and no one dared question his authority.

Living in Rome did not automatically make someone a citizen. All men born in Rome to parents who were citizens themselves could claim that title. Some men who came from communities in Italy that had been conquered were also allowed Roman citizenship. However, women, no matter where they were born or who their parents were, could not claim to be Roman citizens. Slaves could not be citizens, since they were considered to be nothing more than a piece of property, but freed slaves were allowed to become citizens.

c. **82** B.C.
Civil war rages throughout Italy.

c. **82** B.C.
Warriors from the Samnite tribe, from the hills of central Italy, attack Rome but are defeated at the gates by Sulla.

Left: This marble bust shows Jupiter, king of the gods, worshipped by Romans as the holy guardian of their city. When still in his early teens, Caesar was groomed to become Rome's official priest of Jupiter, because of his family's ancient origins. However, changes in the political situation prevented him from taking up his post.

Citizens had many rights and privileges that were not available to noncitizens. They were entitled to vote in elections, choosing the politicians who would represent them. If a citizen committed certain crimes, he would not face the same punishments as a noncitizen. Also, best of all, citizens did not have to pay any taxes. However, freedom had its price. In the early days of the republic, only Roman citizens could join the army, so in times of trouble they were the ones who had to go to war to protect Rome.

The divisions in Roman society did not stop there. There was great conflict between the rich and the poor. There was also conflict between the rich who belonged to the old land-owning families and those who had made their money in other ways. Members of the old, aristocratic families were known as patricians. They could trace their ancestry back to the families who had founded the city. All other citizens were known as plebeians.

82 B.C.
Sulla's political group, the Optimates, persecutes its rivals. Some are exiled while others are murdered.

82 B.C.
Marcus Antonius, who will later become Caesar's loyal friend, is born.

Some plebeians were as rich as most patricians—or even richer. These people had made their fortunes as bankers and merchants. They might not have the noble blood of their patrician neighbors, but they could afford to live just as well. Cossutia, the young girl that Caesar jilted to marry Cornelia, came from one of these families.

All these social groups argued with each other and among themselves. During Gaius's childhood the tensions between citizens and noncitizens had boiled over into the lengthy conflict called the Social War. People from neighboring parts of Italy demanded the right to become Roman citizens. Why should they pay taxes when those living a few miles away paid nothing? In times of war they had been Rome's faithful allies. They were tired of being exploited, so they went to war against Rome itself to prove their point. After many thousands of people died on both sides, the senate finally gave in to the outsiders' demands. Italians from outside Rome could now call themselves Roman citizens.

Above: A wall painting on a tomb shows a young Roman man making a sacrificial offering to the gods.

81 B.C.
Cisalpine Gaul—the northern part of present-day Italy—becomes a province of Rome.

81 B.C.
Sulla becomes dictator and reforms the law to favor the patricians.

Caesar's Choice

Soon after coming of age, Caesar found himself caught up in a power struggle between two opposing factions—the Populares and the Optimates. The Populares favored giving more power to the common people, while the Optimates wanted the senators to stay in control. But their differences went far beyond political disagreements. The two groups hated each other with a murderous passion. At the height of their rivalry, citizens' blood flowed through the streets of Rome.

Above: This bust of Caesar's uncle Gaius Marius (157–86 B.C.) shows the war hero and politician as a man with strong, determined features.

Caesar's family relationships linked him with the Populares. His late uncle Marius had led the faction before his death. Once the old war hero was gone, Caesar's father-in-law, Cinna, had become the Populares' leading light. He secured power for the Populares by ordering a mass slaughter of the Optimates. Then Cinna was assassinated by mutinous troops during a military expedition.

Cinna's enemy, Sulla, was leader of the Optimates. Like Marius, he was a soldier and politician.

81 B.C.
Sulla tries to make Caesar divorce his wife. Caesar refuses.

81 B.C.
Caesar leaves Rome to escape Sulla's anger.

Left: Cicero (106–43 B.C.), portrayed in a bust, was one of the most famous Roman orators. He and Caesar had studied with the same teacher.

At the time of Cinna's death, Sulla had been away in Turkey, fighting a war. Now he marched back into Rome at the head of an army. The senate quickly appointed him dictator to look after their interests.

Sulla ordered Caesar to come before him. He wanted to see his old rival's son-in-law for himself. Caesar's family connections made him a potentially useful tool. He told the young man that he should not abandon his hopes of a political career, even though he had fallen into bad company among the Populares. Sulla told Caesar that he should divorce Cornelia. By breaking off his ties with the hated Cinna's daughter, Caesar would prove his loyalty to Rome and improve his chances of advancement.

Many ambitious young men would have seen this as an easy way to win the approval of the mighty dictator and further their career. However, to Sulla's astonishment, Caesar refused. He saw no reason to send away a beloved wife who was also the mother of his child.

When Caesar told his friends what had happened, they said he was lucky to be alive. Sulla would be a dangerous enemy. Everyone advised him to get out of Rome as fast as possible. The young man said goodbye to his wife and baby daughter, then headed east.

80 B.C.

In Spain, Roman legions who had supported Caesar's late uncle Marius go to war against troops loyal to Sulla.

80 B.C.

Olympia in Greece, sacred site of the Olympic Games for centuries, is plundered by a Roman army.

THE WARRIOR

3

Foreign Adventures

When Julius Caesar hurried out of Rome to escape Sulla's anger, he was also doing what many other young nobles did to launch themselves into their future careers. Those who wanted to serve Rome could join the army as an officer, helping to govern the provinces, or stay at home and help govern the state. Or, best of all, they could do both.

Before he left the city, Caesar was able to get help from influential friends. They arranged for him to travel 2,400 miles (3,862 km) eastward to Asia Minor (part of modern-day Turkey) to join the staff of Marcus Minucius Thermus, who was the Roman military governor for this remote province.

Governors posted to distant places often invited well-educated Roman youths to serve as assistants and companions. Looking after Rome's interests abroad, in peacetime or in war, was a demanding job.

Previous page: This statue of Julius Caesar shows him dressed in the style of a Roman warrior, wearing an ornate metal breastplate.

Left: Made of thousands of tiny tiles in the 1st century A.D., this Roman mosaic shows a slave carrying a dish for a banquet. It was found in the ruined North African city of Carthage, in present-day Tunisia.

c. 80 B.C.
Alexandria in Egypt becomes the center of the east–west spice trade, with its main gate named the Pepper Gate.

c. 80 B.C.
King Mithridates threatens Roman settlements in Asia Minor.

Left: This eagle, carved not long after Caesar's lifetime but set into a frame from the 16th century A.D., carries a wreath of oak leaves, Rome's official badge of honor for military heroes, known as the "civic crown." Caesar was awarded such a wreath for his part in the victory at Mitylene.

There were any number of tasks a bright young man could do to help. Youngsters who would someday go on to run the republic would gain useful military experience and knowledge of the world beyond Rome.

Marcus Minucius Thermus quickly realized that Caesar had a lot to offer. The young man was a gifted communicator and very good with people. He wrote clearly and was an excellent public speaker—not just in his native Latin tongue, but in Greek, which served as the international language for the Mediterranean world at that time.

Caesar was soon entrusted with a very important diplomatic assignment. Marcus Minucius Thermus was engaged in a lengthy war with an enemy of Rome. Mithridates, the king of Pontus, was busy stirring up trouble in territories all around the eastern part of the Mediterranean Sea. Pontus was a kingdom on the northeastern side of Asia Minor, along the southern coast of the Black Sea. Spurred on by King Mithridates, the residents of Mitylene on the Aegean island of Lesbos had launched a rebellion against their Roman overlords.

80 B.C.	80 B.C.
Caesar joins the staff of Marcus Minucius Thermus, Roman military governor in Asia Minor.	Caesar becomes a close friend of King Nicomedes of Bithynia.

Left: A relief carved in the 2nd century A.D. on Trajan's Column in Rome shows ships being propelled through the water by rows of sailors using wooden oars.

To put down this rebellion, Marcus Minucius Thermus needed help from an important ally. Nicomedes was the king of Bithynia, very close to Pontus. Even though he was Mithridates's neighbor, King Nicomedes had sworn loyalty to Rome. He had offered Caesar's boss the loan of his warships to help fight Mithridates. So Marcus Minucius Thermus sent Caesar to Bithynia, to tell its king the time had come to send down his fleet.

The mission was a success. Caesar and King Nicomedes quickly became close friends. Bithynia's ships sailed southward to help the Romans blockade the port of Mitylene. Caesar had his first real taste of combat. He was awarded military honors for his part in conquering the rebel city.

80 B.C.

Caesar wins a wreath known as the "civic crown" after the military victory at Mitylene.

80 B.C.

Cicero launches his career as one of Rome's greatest orators when he defends one of Sulla's political victims in court.

Ransom

The first time Caesar was kidnapped by pirates, he paid a ransom of 25 talents—1,100 pounds—of silver. The second time they demanded twice that amount.

This was only the first of Caesar's many foreign adventures. Over the next few years he would also be captured— twice—by pirates. Travel by sea was always dangerous. Ships, built of wood and powered by sails and oars, were small and fragile. The Mediterranean had frequent storms, many dangerous currents, and hidden rocks that could shred a vessel to splinters. However, travel by road was very slow, so long-distance trips were usually made by faster and easier sea routes. Often traveling by boat was the only way to move between different parts of the far-flung Roman world.

Pirates added to travelers' miseries. They stole cargoes, sold passengers as slaves, and held the rich ones to ransom. As a Roman noble, Caesar was a profitable catch. The first time he was captured, he paid his ransom quickly and went on his way. The second time, his captors demanded twice as much money, and imprisoned him until the gold arrived. At the time, Caesar was on his way to the island of Rhodes to study with a famous teacher of rhetoric.

While he waited for friends back home to receive the message and send a ransom, Caesar teased and joked with the pirates. He told them that he would come back with some warships and capture them in turn. Then he would have them sentenced to death by crucifixion, which was a common means of executing criminals. The pirates thought this was very funny, but later Caesar did exactly what he promised.

79 B.C.
Sulla resigns as dictator.

79 B.C.
Sulla dies.

The Roman Army

The Roman army was one of the most effective and well-organized fighting machines the world has ever known. It enabled Rome to conquer hundreds of different tribes, kingdoms, and even empires across Europe, North Africa, and western Asia, and to hold power over them for centuries.

There were many different reasons why this huge military organization worked so well. In part, Rome had to thank Caesar's late uncle General Marius. Before his time, only Roman citizens who owned land were allowed to fight for the republic. They had to bring along their own weapons, and when the war was over they all went home to plow their fields. Marius turned the army from a loose collection of amateur warriors into a professional fighting force. He invited every Roman citizen—even those too poor to have land of their own—to join. For the first time, every soldier received a regular salary. The army provided soldiers with food, shelter, and all the weapons they needed, and trained every new recruit to make sure he was fit for combat.

Main picture: Soldiers on the march lived in temporary camps. When they stopped for the night, they dug a circular ditch, piled up the earth to build a rough wall, and pitched their tents inside this ring. Later, Roman troops lived in permanent forts, like this one at Portchester, on the southern coast of England, built in the late 3rd century A.D. It was guarded by massive round watchtowers and stone walls 20 feet (6 m) high.

Below: A relief carved on a Roman arch in southern France shows a battle scene in which soldiers are fighting in many different ways and using a variety of weapons. Cavalrymen mounted on huge warhorses aim spears at soldiers engaged in hand-to-hand combat. Helmeted infantrymen swing their swords, which clash against metal shields or cut deep into human flesh left exposed by gaps in someone's armor.

Left: Every Roman soldier was issued weapons and armor. Standard military gear included the items pictured here: a short sword, a shield long and broad enough to cover him from his neck down to his knees, and a metal helmet. A soldier would have also carried a long spear and worn some kind of protective metal breastplate.

Right: The Roman army was organized into large troops, known as legions, each consisting of up to 6,000 men. Every legion had a standard—an eagle, symbol of Roman power, made of gold or silver and mounted on a pole. This bronze figurine from the 1st century A.D. represents the soldier—known as the *aquilifer*—who was responsible for carrying the standard on the march or into battle and holding it high, so that everyone in the legion could follow it. The greatest shame that could befall a legion was the loss of its standard to the enemy.

The Rise to Power

In 78 B.C., news traveled from Rome to Asia Minor that Caesar's dangerous enemy, the former dictator Sulla, was dead. So the 22-year-old Caesar, now a seasoned warrior with a decoration for bravery on his record, felt safe enough to return to Rome.

Soon after coming home, Caesar began to plead legal cases in the Roman courts. This was a good way for young nobles to launch a political career. His quick mind and public-speaking skills helped him win many cases. He became popular among the plebeians when he prosecuted an aristocrat named Dolabella, a politician from Sulla's party who was on trial for corruption. Those Romans who had suffered under Sulla hailed Caesar as a friend of the poor. Caesar began to work his way up the political ladder, serving the government both at home and overseas. He returned to Asia Minor to fight against King Mithridates, and traveled to the western edge of the Roman world to serve as the assistant governor for the province of Further Spain. Later, he would return there to govern the province.

Above: Caesar liked to collect precious objects. Only the richest Romans could have afforded this blown-glass vessel, known today as the Portland Vase.

78 B.C.
Julius Caesar returns to Rome.

77 B.C.
Caesar begins to work in the law courts and successfully prosecutes a provincial governor for corruption.

In 69 B.C. Caesar's wife, Cornelia, died. He soon remarried. His new wife, Pompeia, was Sulla's granddaughter. The marriage did not last long. Caesar heard that Pompeia had misbehaved with another man at a festival. He thought it might ruin his career, so he divorced her, saying, "Caesar's wife must be above suspicion."

Caesar also established a close working relationship with Pompey, a general and former consul, who was one of the most influential men in Rome. When Caesar's daughter, Julia, was in her twenties, he arranged for her to marry Pompey.

In 65 B.C. Caesar became Curule Aedile, the official in charge of public entertainments. He staged exciting spectacles, and the people loved him for it. In 60 B.C., at the age of forty, Julius Caesar was elected to serve as consul. He had support from Pompey and from Crassus, the richest Roman of the day. He promised to run things in a way that would make Pompey even stronger and Crassus even richer.

Above: This bundle of rods, lashed to a metal axe, was called the *fasces*. It was the official symbol of the Roman consuls.

Extravagant spending

Caesar became famous for his love of parties and his expensive tastes. He spent huge amounts of money on luxuries for himself and lavish gifts for his friends. Rumor had it that he once spent a fortune building a brand-new country house, but decided he did not like it and immediately had it torn down.

75 B.C.
Caesar is captured by pirates for the second time.

69 B.C.
Caesar's wife, Cornelia, dies.

The Conqueror of Gaul

After Caesar finished his year-long term as consul, the senate made him military governor of southern Gaul, whose people now lived peaceably with Rome. In 58 B.C., Caesar arrived in Gaul, where he was to spend nine very successful years.

Caesar had four legions under his command in Gaul, guarding against invasion by hostile tribes from farther north. Caesar's political power and public support had made him enemies in Rome—and they were worried. They did not like the idea of this power-hungry general in charge of 20,000 loyal soldiers ready to do anything he wanted—even to march on Rome itself.

Caesar successfully fought off several invasions in Gaul, defeating his attackers by a combination of clever military tactics, careful planning, superior weapons, and good luck. Sometimes he used charm and diplomacy instead of violence. He persuaded one tribal leader that he would be better off if he put himself and his people under Rome's protection. Then he sent him off with a message to other chiefs, inviting them to do the same.

Those tribes who stood against Rome were punished severely, on and off the battlefield.

Left: A coin dating from around 48 B.C. shows Prince Vercingetorix, the last rebel chief defeated by Caesar in Gaul. Caesar admired his courage but brought him back to Rome for execution.

67 B.C.
Caesar marries Pompeia but divorces her in 62 B.C.

65 B.C.
Caesar takes charge of Rome's public entertainments.

Caesar did not spare the lives of women and children. Those he did not put to the sword he sent off under guard to be sold into slavery.

To bring peace to Gaul, Caesar defeated some 300 different tribes, stormed 800 towns, and reckoned that his legions had grappled with around 3 million enemy warriors. By the time the wars were over, all of Gaul—from the northern edges of Italy up through present-day Switzerland, Austria, France, and Belgium—had come under the control of Rome. Within a few generations, the region's inhabitants would be completely absorbed into the Roman world. Their towns would be built in the Roman style; they would speak in the Latin language; and they would worship Roman gods.

Below: This imposing triumphal arch in Orange, France, built in the 1st century A.D., symbolized the power of Rome to the provincial population.

64 B.C.
Under the military command of Pompey, Rome takes control of Syria and moves on to conquer Palestine.

60 B.C.
Caesar is elected as consul in a political alliance with Pompey and Crassus.

Even as he fought them, Caesar was fascinated by the tribes of Gaul. He took notes about their religion, their customs, their clothing, and their daily lives. Later, he published a book about everything he had done and seen. This work, *The Gallic Wars*, is still considered one of the most important history books ever written.

Above: Roman soldiers, carved on Trajan's Column in Rome in A.D. 113, put their engineering skills into practice building a road and a fort.

While in Gaul, Caesar also found time for another adventure. He twice took a fleet of ships across the Channel, which separated the European mainland from the island of Britain. The islanders fought so fiercely against the Romans that Caesar decided the time was not yet right for a full-scale invasion. He ordered his men back to France. It would be another hundred years before the Romans returned.

Wherever Caesar led, his men would gladly follow. He was respected by his soldiers. He worked them hard, but they felt that he treated them fairly.

"His expedition into Britain was the most famous testimony of his courage. For he was the first who brought a fleet into the western ocean, or who sailed into the Atlantic with an army to make war ... and in his attempt to occupy it he carried the Roman empire beyond the limits of the known world."
Plutarch, *A Life of Caesar*, 1st century A.D.

59 B.C.
Caesar's daughter, Julia, marries Pompey.

58 B.C.
Caesar launches a long and successful war to conquer all remaining parts of Gaul.

He also knew how to make the best use of those with special skills. During one battle against a tribe, his men took just a few days to build a bridge strong enough to carry the invasion force across a raging river.

The Romans also used their engineering skills to control the lands they conquered. They developed methods of building excellent roads, making it possible to move men and equipment quickly across vast distances. One of the Romans' most useful inventions was concrete, which was first used in the 2nd century B.C. It was made by combining the ash from volcanoes with water and small stones. The mixture was light and easy to work with, but it set into a material that was almost indestructible, allowing Romans to construct buildings that would last—and are still lasting—for thousands of years.

Below: Still standing high above a deep gorge in southern France, the aqueduct known as the Pont du Gard was built in the 1st century A.D. It carried 20,000 tons of water daily to the Roman city of Nimes.

55 B.C.
Caesar leads Rome's first military expedition to Britain.

55 B.C.
The senate honors Caesar with a formal vote of thanks for his victories.

Caesar Versus Pompey

Caesar and Pompey's friendship was increasingly strained. Although Caesar was still away in Gaul, the two ambitious men were becoming bitter rivals for power. In 54 B.C., Caesar's daughter, Julia, died in childbirth, cutting the final bond between the two men.

During Caesar's years in Gaul, the Roman state lurched from one crisis to another. There were conspiracies against the government, riots in the streets, and politicians murdered by their opponents. Caesar and Pompey, Rome's two greatest warriors, were spoiling for a fight—with each other. To make matters worse, each general had thousands of soldiers under his command who would follow their leader anywhere. The soldiers might be part of the Roman army, but their loyalty was to the man who commanded them in the field.

Right: A marble bust of Caesar's rival, Pompey the Great (106–48 B.C.).

54 B.C.
Caesar's mother, Aurelia, and his daughter, Julia, die.

53 B.C.
Rome is torn apart by political hatred and public riots.

A strange gift

Ptolemy XIII ordered Pompey's murder in the hope of pleasing Caesar. After the murder, Pompey's head was cut off so Ptolemy could present it to Caesar as a gift.

Everyone took sides. The aristocratic Optimates supported Pompey, while the Populares favored Caesar. In late 50 B.C., Caesar declared his plans to run again for the consulship. According to the rules, a candidate could only run for office if he was actually in Rome. The senate also insisted that Caesar give up his military command before the election. Caesar, back in Gaul with his army, refused. The senate sent Caesar a message: Hand over your legions to a new military governor or be condemned for treason. Although some senators supported Caesar, the consul Marcellus invited Pompey to gather troops against Caesar.

Caesar responded by marching a legion south to the Rubicon River, the boundary between Gaul and Italy. He warned his men that, if they did not beat Pompey, they would be executed as traitors. Only one officer, called Labienus, backed down. On the night of January 10, 49 B.C., Caesar's army crossed the river.

Heading south, Caesar met little resistance. Alarmed at the lack of support for their cause, Pompey and the senators who had backed him fled Italy. Before long, Caesar had entered Rome and established his supporters in the senate. Then he set off to fight Pompey.

For 18 months, civil war raged across the Roman world. After defeating Pompey in a battle at Pharsalus in Greece, Caesar chased him south across the Mediterranean Sea to Egypt. However, before Caesar could reach him, Pompey was murdered by order of Ptolemy XIII, the 14-year-old king of Egypt.

January 10, 49 B.C.
Caesar defies the senate's order to surrender his army command and leads his men into Italy.

August 9, 48 B.C.
After 18 months of war, Caesar defeats Pompey in battle at Pharsalus in Greece.

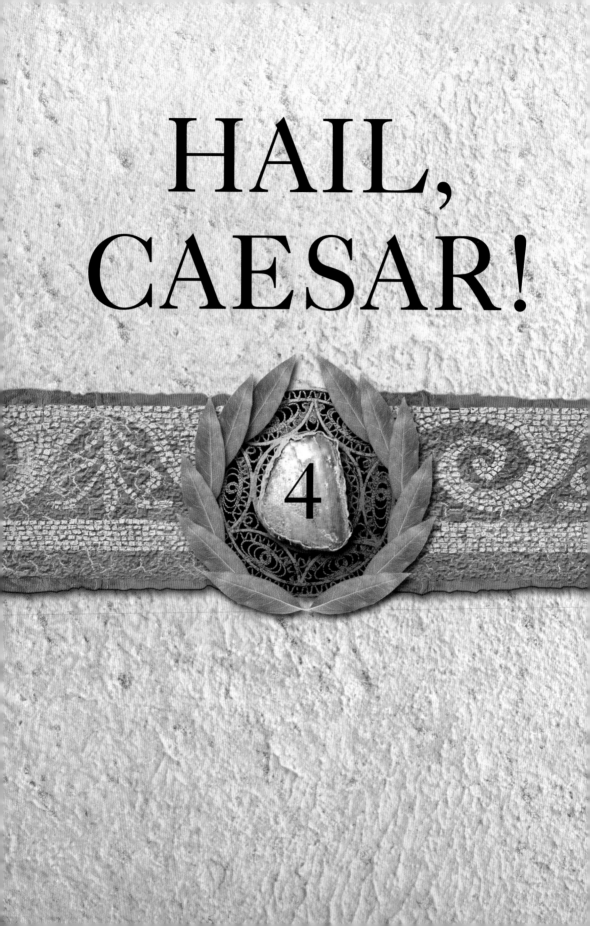

HAIL, CAESAR!

4

Caesar in Egypt

In 48 B.C., Egypt was the richest country in the Mediterranean world. For nearly 300 years, it had been ruled by a family of Greek kings, the Ptolemies. Caesar did not just lead his army to Egypt to capture Pompey: He also wanted to put Egypt under Rome's control.

After Caesar had arrived in Egypt, he saw something that caught his eye: Cleopatra, Ptolemy's 21-year-old sister. She seemed to like Caesar too, even though, at 52, he was more than twice her age. In fact, it was Caesar's support she really wanted. She felt she had as much right to the throne as her brother and wanted Caesar to back her.

Caesar suggested that Ptolemy and Cleopatra should rule together. Ptolemy plotted to kill Caesar, but the plan was discovered. Members of the royal family sided with Ptolemy, along with the citizens of the capital, Alexandria. War broke out. During a battle in Alexandria's harbor, Caesar narrowly escaped death, but Ptolemy drowned.

Previous page: Sculpted in marble, a bust from the 1st century A.D. depicts Julius Caesar as he might have appeared in the prime of life, at the peak of his political career.

Left: A limestone relief on the walls of an Egyptian temple, possibly sculpted in Cleopatra's own lifetime, shows her wearing the crown of an ancient Egyptian queen.

September 28, 48 B.C.
Pompey is murdered by agents of King Ptolemy XIII of Egypt.

October 48 B.C.
Caesar arrives in Alexandria and meets Cleopatra.

Right: Roman soldiers, depicted on a 1st-century B.C. mosaic floor found in a Roman shrine, shelter from the Egyptian sun in a columned temple on the banks of the River Nile.

In June 47 B.C., Caesar sailed out of Alexandria, leaving behind a satisfied Cleopatra. She now ruled Egypt with her one surviving brother, the 11-year-old Ptolemy XIV. The new young king died three years later, perhaps not from natural causes. Not long after Caesar's departure, Cleopatra gave birth to a baby boy. Caesar proudly claimed the child as his son. Caesar also left behind three legions, securing Rome's hold over Egypt.

Luck stayed on Caesar's side. He sailed for Asia Minor to join other Roman forces against King Pharnaces II of Pontus, the son of Mithridates. Until Caesar and his troops arrived in Zela, in what is now eastern Turkey, Pharnaces had had the upper hand. However, once Caesar arrived on the battlefield, it took him only four hours to destroy the army of Pontus. At his triumphal procession to celebrate the victory, soldiers carried placards with the slogan "Veni, Vidi, Vici" ("I came, I saw, I conquered").

"Her tongue, like an instrument with many strings, she could readily turn to whatever language she pleased."
The 1st-century A.D. Roman historian Plutarch on Cleopatra

August 1, 47 B.C.
Caesar defeats Pharnaces at the Battle of Zela.

47 B.C.
Cleopatra gives birth to Caesar's son, Caesarion.

Roman Religion

The Romans believed in dozens of gods and goddesses. Some of their gods were similar to those of ancient Greece. The king of all the gods, for instance, was called Zeus by the Greeks and Jupiter by the Romans. Aphrodite, Greek goddess of love, was similar to the Roman goddess Venus. These immortal beings all had their own special roles and responsibilities, much like the officials who ran the republic. The Romans believed that the gods protected their state. If there was a defeat or a disaster, they believed that they must have annoyed the gods in some way. The Romans built temples to honor their gods, celebrating their festivals on special days every year. Led by priests, they offered up prayers and sacrifices. The priests were chosen from among the leaders of the state: aristocrats, politicians, and soldiers.

Right: The temple of the hearth-goddess, Vesta, built in the 1st century B.C., was one of Rome's holiest places. Inside, a sacred fire was tended 24 hours a day by six priestesses, known as the Vestal Virgins.

Left: Every Roman home had its own private shrine to the household gods, like this one from a 1st-century A.D. house in the Italian town of Pompeii. These gods looked after the family's welfare and made sure that there was always food on the table. As well as offering prayers, Romans would mark special occasions and happy events by placing gifts and treats on their private altars.

Right: This marble statue of Mars, the Roman god of war, was found in Egypt. Like the soldiers Caesar posted there to look after Rome's interests, he wears a helmet and carries a weapon.

Above: A procession of Roman worshippers appears on this relief from the 1st century A.D., leading a pig, a sheep, and an ox as sacrifices. Animals, selected from the finest and fattest on their owners' farms, were slaughtered as gifts to the gods. Their internal organs were removed so priests could study the markings on them, believing these would help them to predict the future. Some of the meat might be set aside for priests to eat.

Caesar Triumphant

When he returned to Rome in 46 B.C., Caesar was full of confidence. With enemies like Pompey and his supporters out of the way, he was about to make his mark on Rome—and Rome seemed willing to let him take power. The senate appointed him dictator for a term of ten years. Surging with the same energy he displayed in battle, he launched into a program of radical changes.

Caesar's first priority was to make sure that no one would stand in his way. He reorganized the senate, expanding its membership to include many of his supporters. The new senators included army veterans who had fought alongside him. They were practical people, with firsthand knowledge of the lands under Rome's control.

Caesar believed that a huge empire needed to be run in a very different way from a tiny city-state. He increased the number of government officials who would help get things done. An important city such as Rome needed to look the part. Caesar built a new senate house, temples, and markets.

Above: To expand the public spaces in his capital, Caesar built a new, elegant forum (pictured here) alongside the forum that had served as the heart of Rome for centuries.

July 25, 46 B.C.
Caesar returns to Rome and is given a ten-year term as dictator.

Autumn 46 B.C.
Caesar reforms the Roman calendar.

Left: According to Roman tradition, the legendary hero of the Trojan War, Aeneas, shown here with a doctor treating his wounds, was the ancestor of Rome's founders. Caesar claimed him as an ancestor, too, as well as the goddess Venus. It was not uncommon for ancient rulers to claim divine ancestors.

Caesar also made sure to please the Roman crowds. He celebrated his many military victories with four spectacular triumphal processions, displaying royal captives from Asia, Africa, and Gaul, and showing off plundered treasures worth the equivalent of around $10 million. He hosted a banquet for 10,000 people and distributed the equivalent of $100 to each Roman citizen, along with generous rations of free grain and oil. He also produced a set of unforgettable spectacles, including staged naval battles with real ships on a specially flooded artificial lake. There were also war games—featuring real deaths—pitting hundreds of condemned criminals against prisoners of war.

Caesar also made his mark with something that would last much longer than the spectacles in the arena. The old Roman calendar had had 355 days per year. Caesar added another ten days and introduced leap years, with 366 days, every four years. This was to take into account the fact that the earth actually moves round the sun once every 365.24 days. We still use this system today, and one of our months, July, is named after Caesar.

October 45 B.C.
The senate makes Caesar dictator for life.

45 B.C.
Caesar's statues are placed in Rome's holiest temples.

Murder

In 45 B.C., the senate voted Caesar dictator for life. He began to act like a king instead of a servant of the republic. He presided over the senate sitting on a golden throne. His statues were placed in Rome's holiest temples, right next to images of the gods themselves. Coins appeared bearing Caesar's face—the first time in Rome's history that any living person had been given this honor. People were afraid to oppose him.

Caesar's former supporters and his old enemies began to find things in common. Even his friends whispered behind his back about his hunger for power. Public-spirited Romans feared for the republic's future. Senators could see the day coming when they would be nothing but puppets, stripped of the authority they had held for centuries. Quietly, among those they trusted, a handful of leading citizens agreed that there was only one way to stop the tyrant: Caesar had to die.

Sixty people came together to plan the murder. Their two leaders were Cassius and Brutus. Both had fought on Pompey's side against Caesar. Like many other allies of Pompey, they had been pardoned by Caesar and promoted to high office. Caesar was said to be especially fond of Brutus. There were even rumors that Brutus was his son.

Above: A bronze bust shows Brutus (c. 85–42 B.C.), a ringleader of the plot to kill Caesar.

45 B.C.
Caesar's face begins to appear on Roman coins.

February 15, 44 B.C.
Caesar makes a public appearance wearing the traditional robes of the ancient kings of Rome.

The plotters decided to kill Caesar at the senate. This was the one place in Rome where they could all appear without causing suspicion. The senate was due to meet next on March 15, the day known as the Ides of March. According to Roman historians, a fortune-teller named Spurinna warned the dictator to beware of some danger on that date. Caesar did not need a fortune-teller to see trouble brewing. He believed that Rome could only survive under a strong leader, but he knew he was playing a dangerous game.

When Caesar entered the senate on March 15, 44 B.C., a crowd rushed up and surrounded him. Appalled to see Brutus among his attackers, Caesar is said to have called out to him, "Even you, my child!" Within moments Caesar lay dead, with 23 stab wounds in his body.

Below: The death of Julius Caesar, one of the most famous moments in Roman history, is portrayed in a 1793 painting by Italian artist Vincenzo Camuccini.

An unexpected death

According to the historian Plutarch, Julius Caesar was at a dinner party where the guests asked each other what kind of death was best. Caesar's answer was "an unexpected one."

End February–early March 44 B.C.
Sixty conspirators meet in secret to plot Caesar's murder.

March 15, 44 B.C.
Caesar is stabbed to death at a meeting of the senate.

Caesar's Legacy

The horrified people of Rome came in the thousands to Caesar's funeral in the forum. As the smoke rose over the funeral pyre, the crowd was overcome and started throwing tributes to Caesar into the flames. Old soldiers flung in their weapons; women sacrificed their jewels; actors and musicians tore off their costumes and ran naked through the streets.

In his will, Caesar gave each Roman family a large sum of money. Since he had no legitimate son, in his will Caesar also adopted his great-nephew Octavian, his sister Julia's grandson, as his official son and heir. After a period of civil war, Octavian gained control of the empire in 27 B.C., becoming the first true Roman emperor (from the Latin for "supreme commander"). Octavian took complete power and ended the democratic days of the republic forever—exactly what Caesar's assassins had been trying to prevent.

Below: Built in the 2nd century A.D., Hadrian's Wall in Britain marked the northern limit of the Roman Empire.

27 B.C.

Caesar's great-nephew Octavian becomes the first Roman emperor, taking the name Augustus Caesar.

A.D. 117

The Roman Empire reaches its largest extent, from Britain in the northwest to Dacia and Parthia in the east.

Without Julius Caesar's military victories and political vision, the Roman world might never have developed in the way it did. At the empire's peak, 60 million people came together to create one of the most inventive civilizations ever known. The Latin spoken in Rome would become an international language, allowing knowledge and ideas—including Christianity—to flow freely across the known world.

As well as making history, Julius Caesar helped record it. His fascinating writings are still important sources of information about the Roman Republic and the lives of the peoples of western Europe in Roman times. Caesar valued learning and respected wisdom. In the last year of his life, he ordered that libraries should be established in every large town under Roman control.

Caesar was regarded as a loyal friend, and he took satisfaction in forgiving many of his political enemies. Although he was an aristocrat, his soldiers and the humbler citizens of Rome regarded him as a man of the people, who respected individuals for their own actions rather than their background or birthplace. However, Caesar liked money and power. He became a ruthless leader, unable to tolerate any challenge to his way of doing things.

His friends and his enemies agreed: Gaius Julius Caesar was no ordinary human being. His words and deeds would inspire political leaders, generals, artists, and authors for thousands of years to come.

Right: Completed in A.D. 79, the vast arena in Rome known as the Colosseum still survives as an enduring symbol of Rome's power.

A.D. **476**
The Roman Empire falls in the west, but in the east, it survives as the Byzantine Empire for another 1,000 years.

c. A.D. **1600**
The world-famous English playwright William Shakespeare writes *The Tragedy of Julius Caesar.*

Glossary

allies people or countries working together or fighting on the same side.

altar a table used in religious ceremonies for making sacrifices or offerings to the gods.

amphitheater a theater used to stage gladiator contests or other spectacles.

aristocrat a member of an old and often wealthy ruling family.

citizen a member of a state who owes loyalty to the government and is entitled to certain rights and protection. In Rome, all free men born in the city were citizens, as well as freed slaves and some members of conquered Italian states.

consul either of two annually elected officials who together held the highest authority in the Roman Republic.

crucified executed by hanging on a cross.

democratic governed by the people or their elected representatives.

dictator ruler who has either taken or been given complete control of a government. In Rome, dictators were appointed by the senate in times of conflict. They were given almost total power, for a period of time.

diplomacy the effort to create good relationships between two different countries—sometimes to prevent a war.

dynasty a family of rulers that passes its power down from one generation to the next.

emperor the supreme ruler of an empire.

execution the act of killing a person by order of the state.

exploited taken advantage of, or used.

forum a large open space, used for meetings, ceremonies, and other public activities.

fresco a picture created by applying paint to a freshly plastered wall. The colors are absorbed by the wet plaster as it dries to create a long-lasting image.

funeral pyre the fire used to burn a dead body as part of a funeral ceremony.

Gaul lands to the north and west of Italy inhabited by a group of Celtic people called the Gallic tribes or the Gauls.

gladiator a prisoner or a slave given weapons and forced to fight—and possibly die—in contests and staged battles. These battles were presented to the Roman public as a form of entertainment.

jilt to reject or leave a lover, usually without giving any warning.

legion a unit of the Roman army, made up of 5,000 to 6,000 fighting men.

legitimate born to married parents.

mosaic a picture created by piecing together thousands of small pieces of colored glass, stone, or tile. Mosaics were used by the Romans to decorate floors and other surfaces.

mythology a collection of ancient stories, often about gods, goddesses, and powerful or superhuman heroes. These stories are used by a people to express its religious beliefs, to explain the origins of the world and everything in it, and to preserve ideas or memories from the distant past.

noble a member of a powerful land-owning family.

offspring sons and daughters—can be used for a single child or many.

Optimates A Roman political group favoring the interests of the old and often wealthy noble families.

orator a person skilled in the art of public speaking.

papyrus an ancient writing material—an early form of paper, made from a reed-like plant, called papyrus, that grew in Egypt along the River Nile.

patrician a member of one of Rome's old land-owning families.

plebeian a member of a Roman family that did not have noble blood. The term was used to describe those Romans who, whether they were poor or not, were considered part of the "common people."

Populares a Roman political group wanting to give more power to ordinary people.

prosecute to accuse a person of a crime and to present evidence about this before a court of law.

ransom a sum of money demanded by kidnappers to release a person they have taken hostage.

reign to rule, in the manner of a king or queen.

relief a kind of carving that projects forward from a flat surface.

republic a country not ruled by a king or queen, but governed by officials elected or appointed by all or some of the people who live there.

rhetoric the art of public speaking.

sacrifice a valuable piece of property or an animal that is offered as a gift to please the gods.

scroll a roll of papyrus or some other early form of paper, with writing on it.

supreme highest, most powerful.

traitor a person who betrays or harms their own community or country.

tribune a Roman official appointed by the people to represent their interests; also, a high-ranking army officer.

triumphal arch a giant stone archway, usually decorated with carvings, set up along the route for a procession—known as a Triumph—held to honor a Roman general who has won a great victory.

Trojan War a war, believed to have been fought in the very remote past, between the Greek city-states and a city called Troy in Asia Minor. According to Roman legend, after Troy was defeated and destroyed, its hero Aeneas founded Rome.

tunic a piece of clothing made from two long pieces of wool or other cloth stitched together.

Bibliography

Ancient Rome: Eyewitness Guide, James, Simon, published by Dorling Kindersley in association with the British Museum, 1990

Caesar, Cawthorne, Nigel, published by Haus Publishing, 2005

Caesar: Life of a Colossus, Goldsworthy, Adrian, published by Weidenfeld & Nicolson, 2006

The Civil War, Caesar, Julius, translated by Carter, John, published by Oxford University Press, 1997

Everyday Life in Ancient Rome, Grant, Neil, published by the British Museum Press, 2003

Readings in the Classical Historians, Grant, Michael, published by Charles Scribner & Sons, 1992

The Roman Family, Vasari Dixon, Suzanne, published by Johns Hopkins University Press, 1992

The Roman Household: A Sourcebook, Gardener, James, and Wiedemann, Thomas, published by Routledge, 1991

Rome: Echoes of Imperial Glory, by the editors of Time-Life Books, published by Time-Life Books, 1994

The Twelve Caesars, Suetonius, translated by Graves, Robert, published by Penguin Books, 1979

The Usborne Internet-Linked Encyclopedia of the Roman World, Chandler, Fiona, Taplin, Sam, and Bingham, Jane, published by Usborne Publishing, 2001

Sources of quotes:

p. 21 Suetonius, *Julius Caesar 45*, quoted in Grant, Michael, p. 511

p. 41 Plutarch, *Life of Caesar*, from *Roman Lives*, Oxford World Classics, 1999

p. 44 Plutarch, *Life of Caesar*

p. 51 Plutarch, *Life of Antony*, quoted in Cawthorne, Nigel, p. 75

p. 57 Both quotes: Plutarch, *Life of Caesar*

Some Web sites that will help you to explore Julius Caesar's world:

www.bbc.co.uk/history/ancient/romans/
www.thebritishmuseum.ac.uk/world/rome/
empire.html
www.hadrians.com
www.historylink102.com/Rome/index.htm
www.roman-empire.net

Index

Acknowledgments

Source: AA = The Art Archive.

B = bottom, C= center, L = left, R = right, T = top.

Front cover © 1990, Photo Scala, Florence – courtesy of the Ministero Beni e Att. Culturali; **1** AA/Jan Vinchon Numismatist, Paris/Dagli Orti; **3** AA/National Archaeological Museum, Chieti/Dagli Orti; **4T** AA/ Musée du Louvre, Paris/Dagli Orti; **4B** AA/Museo della Civilta Romana, Rome/Dagli Orti; **5T** TopFoto; **5B** © 1990, Photo Scala, Florence – courtesy of the Ministero Beni e Att. Culturali; **7, 9** AA/Musée du Louvre, Paris/Dagli Orti; **10** AA/Museo della Civilta Romana, Rome/Dagli Orti; **11** AA/Musée du Louvre, Paris/Dagli Orti; **12** © 2003, Photo Scala, Florence – courtesy of the Ministero Beni e Att. Culturali; **13** Werner Forman Archive/Museo Archeologico Nazionale, Naples; **14T** AA/Dagli Orti; **14B** © 1990, Photo Scala, Florence; **15T** AA/Archaeological Museum, Naples/Dagli Orti; **15B** Werner Forman Archive/ Metropolitan Museum of Art, New York; **16** AA/Musée du Louvre, Paris/Dagli Orti; **17** AA/Museo Nazionale Terme, Rome/Dagli Orti; **19** AA/Museo della Civilta Romana, Rome/Dagli Orti; **20** AA/Museo Opitergino Oderzo, Treviso/Dagli Orti; **21** AA/Dagli Orti; **22** John Parker; **23** © Gianni Dagli Orti/Corbis; **24** Werner Forman Archive/J. Paul Getty Museum, Malibu; **25** AA/Archaeological Museum, Naples/ Dagli Orti; **26** AA/Archaeological Museum, Florence/Dagli Orti; **27** AA/Jan Vinchon Numismatist, Paris/Dagli Orti; **28** AA/Museo Nazionale Palazzo Altemps, Rome/Dagli Orti; **29** Werner Forman Archive; **30, 31** AA/Museo della Civilta Romana, Rome/Dagli Orti; **33** TopFoto; **34** akg-images/Erich Lessing; **35** akg-images/Nimatallah; **36** AA/Museo della Civilta Romana, Rome/Dagli Orti; **38–39, 39T** John Parker; **39CL** © 1990, Photo Scala, Florence – courtesy of the Ministero Beni e Att. Culturali; **39BR** AA/National Archaeological Museum, Chieti/Dagli Orti; **40** © 2003, Photo Scala, Florence/HIP; **41, 42** akg-images; **43** John Parker; **44** akg-images; **45** John Parker; **46** AA/Archaeological Museum, Venice/Dagli Orti; **49** © 1990, Photo Scala, Florence – courtesy of the Ministero Beni e Att. Culturali; **50** AA; **51** AA/Museo Prenestino, Palestrina/Dagli Orti; **52** © Robert Harding World Imagery/Corbis; **53TL** Werner Forman Archive; **53CR** AA/Musée du Louvre, Paris/Dagli Orti; **53B** AA/Archaeological Museum, Alexandria/Dagli Orti; **54** Hervé Champollion/akg-images; **55** © 1990, Photo Scala, Florence – courtesy of the Ministero Beni e Att. Culturali; **56** AA/Museo della Civilta Romana, Rome/Dagli Orti; **57** AA/Galleria d'Arte Moderna, Rome/Dagli Orti; **58** John Parker; **59** Werner Forman Archive.